What Was the Alamo?

by Pam Pollack and Meg Belviso

illustrated by David Groff

Grosset & Dunlap
An Imprint of Penguin Group (USA) Inc.

For Charlie Taylor, silver of tongue, noble of deed—PP

To T.R. & Fran, always up for a fandango—MB

To my wife, Cheryl—DG

GROSSET & DUNLAP
Published by the Penguin Group
Penguin Group (USA) Inc., 375 Hudson Street, New York, New York 10014, USA

USA | Canada | UK | Ireland | Australia | New Zealand | India | South Africa | China
Penguin Books Ltd, Registered Offices: 80 Strand, London WC2R 0RL, England

For more information about the Penguin Group visit penguin.com

Text copyright © 2013 by Pam Pollack and Meg Belviso. Illustrations copyright © 2013 by Penguin Group (USA) Inc. All rights reserved. Published by Grosset & Dunlap, a division of Penguin Young Readers Group, 345 Hudson Street, New York, New York 10014. GROSSET & DUNLAP is a trademark of Penguin Group (USA) Inc. Printed in the U.S.A.

Library of Congress Cataloging-in-Publication Data is available.

ISBN 978-0-448-46710-8   10 9 8

Contents

What Was the Alamo?

In downtown San Antonio, Texas, sit the ruins of an old church. It is crowded in among office buildings, hotels, and shops. This is all that remains of an old Spanish mission.

In the 1700s, missions were where Catholic priests lived and prayed. They also tried to teach their religion to tribes of Native Americans. But the tribes had no interest. By 1793, the mission had been turned into a fort known as the Alamo. (In Spanish, *álamo* means "cottonwood tree"; the name refers to a company of soldiers that had been stationed there.)

The front of the church appears very ordinary. But if you look closely at the white walls, you may find the scars from bullets and cannonballs fired more than 175 years ago. They are from a terrible battle that was fought here in March 1836. Today, over 2.5 million people come to visit each year. Many think of the Alamo as the "cradle of Texas liberty."

Why? What does the Alamo mean to the people of Texas, and to the rest of the United States?

CHAPTER 1
Come and Take It

Since the 1500s, when Spanish explorers first came to the New World, Spain had ruled Mexico. By 1820, Mexico had spread down through Central America, up as far north as present-day Oregon, and all the way to the west coast of North America. It included a huge chunk of land called Texas that shared borders with Louisiana.

In 1821, Mexico won its independence. It no longer belonged to Spain. There was a new government with a constitution. The Mexican Constitution was based in part on the US Constitution and granted many of the same rights, including the right to elect members of the government and the right of the states to govern themselves.

Spanish Territory/
Mexico

Louisiana

Alabama

Tennessee

Very quickly, English-speaking settlers from the southern United States—from Louisiana, Tennessee, and Alabama—came flooding into Texas. Buying land there was cheap—as low as four cents an acre. People in the United States were said to have caught "Texas fever."

At first, Mexico didn't mind the arrival of American settlers. The country needed more people to help defend it against frequent attacks from Native American tribes such as the Comanche and Apache. The Mexicans, however, had a few rules: The settlers from the United States had to become Catholic. They had to swear to be faithful to the country of Mexico. Also, slavery was not allowed in Mexico.

The trouble was that Texians, as these English-speaking settlers were called, didn't like to follow rules. Some brought slaves along and intended to keep them. The settlers didn't want to become Catholic. All they wanted was the chance to own land. There was plenty of that in Texas. So they made Mexico their home. They put down roots.

In time, some Texians came to think of themselves as citizens of Mexico. Some married Tejanos—native Spanish-speaking Mexicans— and had families.

In 1832, things changed. A Mexican general named Antonio López de Santa Anna grabbed control of the government. He had been a hero in Mexico's war for independence against Spain. Now he tossed aside the Mexican Constitution. Santa Anna declared even "a hundred years to come my people will not be fit for liberty," and made himself dictator. When he took control, several states rebelled—and Santa Anna used force to stop the rebellions and punish the states.

In Texas, both Texians and Tejanos were divided over what to do about Santa Anna. Some Texians, like Stephen F. Austin, favored Texas remaining part of Mexico. They hoped in time Santa Anna would become more reasonable and let go of power. Others, such as Sam Houston, wanted war. They thought Texas had to break free from Mexico and Santa Anna. They wanted independence.

Stephen F. Austin

In 1821, Moses Austin had a dream to bring his family and three hundred other settlers to Texas from Missouri. When Moses died, his son Stephen led the new settlers into Texas, where they started

a settlement called San Felipe de Austin. Eventually Austin would bring fifteen hundred families into Texas. For a long time, Austin was loyal to the Mexican government. In 1833, worried about other Texians' growing demands for Texas independence, he went to the government in Mexico City. He asked for Texas to become an independent state that would stay under Mexican rule. Not only was his request denied, but Austin was also arrested. Austin stayed in jail for twelve months. Then he was paroled, but not allowed to go home for another seven months. He left Mexico City a changed man. He said, "Every man in Texas is called to take up arms in defense of his country and his rights." Today he is known as the Father of Texas. The city of Austin is named after him.

Trouble was brewing in many towns. In Gonzales it boiled over.

The early days in Gonzales had been tough. But by 1835, Gonzales had begun to prosper. There were two small hotels, two blacksmith shops, and several bars. A new schoolhouse was being built, and a man named Almeron Dickinson had opened a hat shop. Native American attacks were not as frequent. The town had even held its first fancy ball.

The citizens of Gonzales had not wanted a war
for Texas independence. However, they resented
the way they were treated by Santa Anna's soldiers.
The soldiers were lawless. They were bullies. One
soldier beat up a man with the butt of his gun.

Sam Houston

Sam Houston stood about six feet four inches tall. He cut quite a figure, especially when in the Native American or Mexican clothes that he liked to wear.

He became a hero in the War of 1812 and later a lawyer. He served two terms in the US Congress before being elected governor of Tennessee in 1827. He first saw Texas in 1832 and fell in love with it. Houston struggled with drinking and drug problems throughout his life. The Cherokee, who considered him a friend, called him *Oo-tse-tee Ar-dee-tah-skee,* or "Big Drunk."

Four days before the Alamo massacre, he signed the Texas Declaration of Independence. It said Texas was free from Mexico. After the territory won its independence, he was elected president of the Republic of Texas twice. When Texas became a state, he served from 1846 to 1859 as one of its senators, and after that as its governor. The city of Houston, Texas, is named after him.

Then one day, more soldiers arrived with an empty oxcart. They demanded the town's cannon. The message was clear: No one was allowed to have weapons except Santa Anna's army.

It wasn't much of a cannon. Just a six-pounder. That meant it shot small cannonballs weighing six pounds each. The cannon did little more than make a loud noise and belch smoke. However, the people of Gonzales refused to give up the cannon. They were taking a stand.

The soldiers rode away, but the townspeople knew they would be back. They sent out a call for help to other towns nearby. They needed more people to defend themselves against the soldiers.

When Santa Anna's troops returned to Gonzales, about 140 men were ready to defend the cannon and the town. One young woman is said to have offered up her wedding dress to make into a flag. The flag showed a cannon and the words COME AND TAKE IT. This was like a dare to the soldiers.

Texian James C. Neill fired the first cannon shot. After a quick skirmish, Santa Anna's soldiers retreated. The fighting at Gonzales wasn't even a real battle. It was all over so quickly. Yet this day—October 2, 1835—was the beginning of the war for Texas independence.

CHAPTER 2
The Army of the People

The rebels fighting for freedom called themselves the Army of the People. They were all volunteers and elected Stephen F. Austin as their leader. By now Austin had changed his mind about war. Why?

In 1834, Austin was thrown in jail. All he had done was ask if Texas could become more independent. The answer was no. Austin then wrote a letter to warn his fellow Texians about the Mexican government's hostility, and for that he was imprisoned.

The Army of the People under Austin marched from Gonzales toward the town of San Antonio de Béxar, or Béxar for short. (Today it is known as the city of San Antonio.) In Béxar, the rebel army planned to face off against Santa Anna's troops stationed there.

At that point the army included about three hundred men: a ragtag bunch of farmers, shopkeepers, and craftsmen. They hoped to pick up more volunteers on the way. Few had military training. They had no uniforms—they wore buckskin breeches, shoes or moccasins, sombreros, top hats, or coonskin caps. They rode American horses and Spanish ponies, mustangs and mules.

On October 27, 1835, the army arrived outside Béxar. Many thought it was the prettiest spot in Texas they'd ever seen. About sixteen hundred people lived there, mostly Tejanos. The bell tower of the Church of San Fernando rose up between the two town squares. Beyond the town center were mud and stick shacks, and then cornfields. To the east, across the San Antonio River, was the Alamo. About 650 Mexican soldiers were stationed there and in the town. Their leader was General Martín Perfecto de Cós. He was Santa Anna's brother-in-law.

Inside the Alamo, the soldiers had built a ramp and a platform on what was left of the dome of the Alamo church. They placed cannons there that could fire over the church itself. They had also blocked off streets and set up five cannons in the town squares.

The Army of the People didn't plan on attacking Béxar. That did not seem possible. Instead, Austin and his men settled in for a siege. A siege is when forces surround an enemy and wait them out.

In time the enemy's food and supplies will run out and they will have to surrender. For weeks the Army of the People waited, growing more and more undisciplined. Many lost patience and went home to their families. They were replaced, however, by new arrivals from the United States eager to fight and to win themselves land in Texas.

Winter arrived, bringing cold weather and sickness. Stephen F. Austin, who was among the sick, had to travel to the United States to ask for money for the Texian rebels. That left the Army of the People without the popular Austin as leader.

By December, it seemed as if the siege would be called off. Then Texian rebel Ben Milam rode to Béxar. Originally from Kentucky, he'd been a US soldier. He'd fought in the War of 1812, and he was ready to fight again. Milam galloped up to the men and shouted, "Who will go with old Ben Milam" and fight? Milam was just the kind of man the rebel soldiers needed to fire them up. About three hundred men in the army rushed to join him.

At five o'clock in the morning on December 5, 1835, the battle in Béxar began. Milam's men ran through the cornfields into Béxar. The Mexican artillery opened fire with clouds of grapeshot (clusters of small iron balls). The Mexican soldiers were in uniform and looked like a real army. But most of the soldiers had a gun called the Brown Bess. It was heavy, took a long time to reload, and wasn't accurate. The Mexican gunpowder was often so weak that musket balls sometimes just bounced off the Texians.

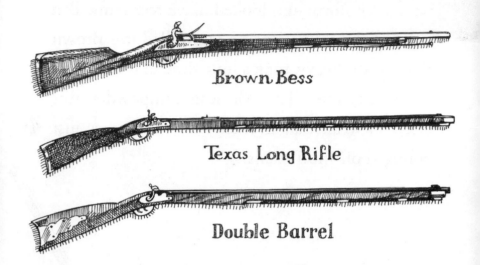

Brown Bess

Texas Long Rifle

Double Barrel

The Brown Bess was no match for the Texians' long rifles and double-barreled shotguns, which were easier to fire and more accurate. The long rifle also had a much longer range—as far as two hundred yards, twice as long as the Brown Bess's one hundred yards.

In Béxar, the rebel army moved from house to house. About 135 Tejanos also joined in the fight. In some homes, the rebels only found scared

Béxar residents who fled in their pajamas. But in some buildings they found Mexican soldiers. Then fighting would break out with pistols and knives and sometimes bare fists.

The fighting went on for five days. Both sides were exhausted. Ben Milam was killed. About three hundred Mexican soldiers had deserted. General Cós ordered all his remaining troops inside the Alamo. That was a mistake. There was no food or water and no way to defend the fort for any length of time. Cós was ready to surrender.

So the general and his men left on December 15, 1835. The Texians allowed them to keep some of their guns and ammunition, and even gave them a cannon. That way the Mexicans

could defend against Native American attacks on the way home.

The Army of the People had won Béxar. The Alamo was theirs. Only five rebels had been killed; about 150 Mexican troops were dead. The rebels were sure they'd seen the last of the Mexican army until spring at least.

They were wrong.

CHAPTER 3
Rumors

The fighting was over for now—that's the way it seemed to the Army of the People. Many returned to their families for planting season.

Others left to help capture Matamoros, a Mexican port city. They marched out of the Alamo, taking horses, food, ammunition, clothing, blankets, and medical supplies. Among the rebels who stayed, discipline was a problem. They were bored, which led to drinking, gambling, and dancing the night away at fandangos (parties).

In January, there was an alarming rumor. Santa Anna was returning to Béxar with a large army. The Mexicans were not waiting until spring to fight. They had started from Satillo, 350 miles away. On hearing the news, people in Béxar started to leave town.

On January 19, a small group of about thirty more rebels arrived at Béxar. They were wet, dirty, and tired. A man named Jim Bowie was among them.

Bowie had been securing troops at a nearby fort in Goliad, Texas. Bowie, however, had not come to help defend the Alamo. His order from Sam Houston was to destroy it.

Houston did not think the Alamo could be held by the Texian soldiers. It had not been built as a fort.

It was not on high ground. It was out in the middle of the fields. That made it hard to defend.

The Alamo also covered a large area—about

three acres. The walls were made of adobe, a mixture of straw and mud. They could withstand Native American arrows, but not cannon fire.

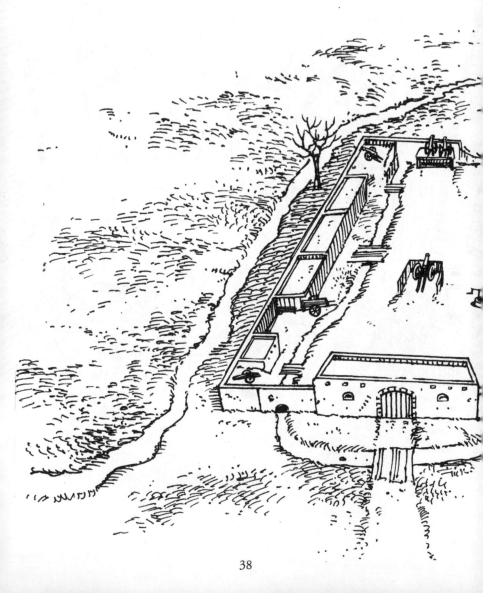

Sooner or later the rebels would be forced to surrender. So Houston wanted to move the cannons out and then destroy the buildings.

By the time Bowie arrived, James Neill, now the leader at the Alamo, had begun to think this was the best plan.

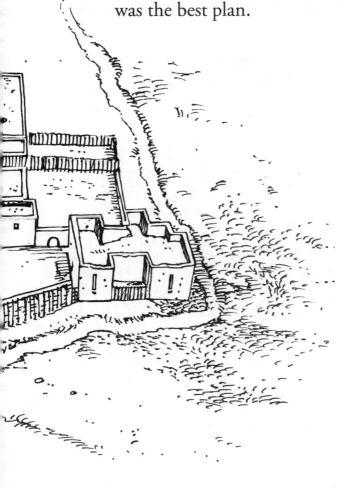

Jim Bowie

"Jim Bowie, Jim Bowie. He was a fighter, a fearless and mighty adventuring man." So went the theme song of the 1950s TV show based on Jim Bowie's life.

Jim Bowie grew up in the tough sugarcane region of Louisiana. He and his older brother learned to shoot deer, trap bears, break mustangs, and even ride alligators. When Bowie grew up, he made a lot of money in shady dealings in the slave trade and land purchases. He was six feet tall and a good fighter. He was a big drinker, too, and known for picking fights. He once murdered a man with the special hunting knife he carried. It became known as a Bowie knife. He moved to Texas and married into a Tejano family. He loved Texas and Mexican culture. Even after the death of his wife and children, he remained in Béxar until his own death at the Alamo.

Before leveling the buildings, Jim Bowie took a tour of the fort. He listened to one of the rebels there who had drawn up plans for repairing the Alamo and turning it into what he called a mighty fortress. The man was not a trained engineer or a military tactician. The plans were only a dream, but they excited Jim Bowie—James Neill, too. There were twenty or so cannons inside the walls. One was a big eighteen-pounder.

That could take out a lot of enemy soldiers. Perhaps repairs could be made, and the rebels could defend the Alamo against a Mexican army, at least until more and better-equipped troops arrived.

Jim Bowie also had a personal reason for wanting to save the Alamo. He felt sentimental about it because he had lived in Béxar for several years. He had married a Tejano woman, and they had two children together. Sadly, his family had died of a disease called cholera. However, Jim Bowie still had friends and family in town. Some of them had helped the Texians during the earlier fight against Cós's army. When the next attack came, Bowie was counting on these families to help again.

So Bowie changed his mind. He decided to disobey Sam Houston's order. He would remain with the other Texians and fight Santa Anna's forces. Jim Bowie decided he was never going to give up the Alamo, not even if it meant dying there.

The Alamo

The Alamo was not just one building. It was a compound, or collection of buildings surrounded by walls that varied in height from nine to twelve feet. Parts of the outer wall had built-in stone rooms. To the left of the main gateway was the Mission Square, a courtyard with barracks at one end. Cannons were located at several points along the walls that surrounded the Mission Square. To the right of the main gateway were other buildings, including the chapel. It had its own courtyard. The roof of the chapel had caved in, but still offered enough support for cannons to be placed on top of it. Beside the chapel were pens for cattle and a horse corral. There were also the long barracks, two stories of rooms that housed soldiers and served as a hospital to tend sick and injured rebels.

Prison

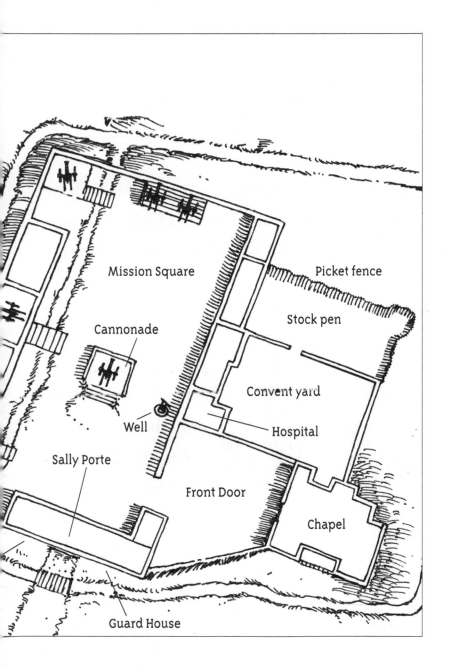

Mission Square

Picket fence

Cannonade

Stock pen

Convent yard

Well

Hospital

Sally Porte

Front Door

Chapel

Guard House

CHAPTER 4
Who Is in Command?

On February 3, twenty-six-year-old William Travis arrived at the Alamo. Originally from Alabama, he had left behind a pregnant wife and a baby boy and made his way to Texas. At his side was a young slave named Joe.

Travis believed in an independent Texas with all his heart. Not only did he want to join the men at the Alamo, he thought he should be their leader. He was a trained soldier, a lieutenant—

not a volunteer like the men in the Army of the People. However, Travis had more experience reading about battles in the pages of novels than actually leading them. He had tried to raise a large group to accompany him to the Alamo but had gathered only about thirty men.

Most of the rebels didn't care much for Travis, who insisted on strict discipline. He wasn't nearly as popular as Jim Bowie or another man who showed up a few days later. His name was David Crockett, a man known as an expert shot with a rifle. In buckskin clothes and a fur hat, Crockett arrived with a group called the Tennessee Mounted Volunteers. They, too, were ready to defend the Alamo.

William Travis

William Barret Travis came to Texas from Alabama to open a law practice. He promised to send for his wife and child but never did. In Texas he had love affairs with many women. He even kept a diary where he wrote all about his romances. Travis was only twenty-six when he took command of the Alamo. He saw himself as a great leader, but his big ego often got in his way. His own men didn't like him much. At the Alamo, David Crockett was much more popular. Although Travis longed for fame, at the time of his death, reports about the Alamo in US newspapers spelled his name wrong.

David Crockett

In the 1950s, Walt Disney aired a wildly popular TV series called *The Adventures of Davy Crockett*. It started a fad for coonskin caps. Kids carried Davy Crockett lunch boxes and knew all the words to the theme song. With dark hair and piercing blue eyes, the real Crockett was a fiercely independent man. In 1826 he was elected to Congress as US representative for Tennessee. He served for three terms. Unlike a lot of politicians at the time, Crockett was against slavery. He also opposed the harsh treatment of Native Americans by the US government. That is pretty amazing considering the fact that his grandparents had been killed in an attack by Creek Indians.

David Crockett was a superstar. There were stories claiming that he'd killed more than a hundred bears in one season and that he could "whip his weight in wildcats."

Amid the cheers of the people of Béxar, Crockett climbed onto a crate in the main square and said, "Fellow citizens, I am among you. . . . I have come to aid you all that I can in your noble cause."

A few days later, on February 11, James Neill had to return home because of an illness in his family. Promising to return soon, Neill left William Travis in charge. That was okay with David Crockett. But Jim Bowie could not accept Travis as leader. Travis was far younger (Jim Bowie was forty) and not nearly as experienced a fighter. Travis demanded that the matter of leadership be put to a vote among all the men. Bowie agreed and won easily. However, he realized that a bitter Travis could cause trouble later on. The men at the Alamo needed to remain united. Also, Jim Bowie had fallen ill. He had been in good health when he first arrived, but now he had come down with a strange sickness. He had fevers. He was growing weaker. (To this day, nobody knows exactly what Jim Bowie was suffering from.) So it made good sense for Bowie to agree to share command at the Alamo with Travis.

On the evening of February 20, word came from a Tejano scout: Santa Anna's army had crossed the Rio Grande! That was only 150 miles away. Santa Anna could be there within days. Was it true? Could the enemy be this close? Travis sent his own scouts to find out more.

While waiting for their return, the men in the Alamo decided to hold a fandango. It was to celebrate George Washington's birthday.

The rebels partied hard all night, dancing and drinking. Many didn't stumble into bed until dawn. They knew that this might be their last chance to have fun for a long time. They knew they might die soon.

They were right.

CHAPTER 5
Bloodred Banner

That afternoon, a Texian lookout began ringing the Béxar church bell. The enemy was in sight! Some citizens in Béxar called out to the Texians, "Poor fellows, you will all be killed!" A few of the townspeople, however, decided to seek safety inside the Alamo. Among them were Jim Bowie's sisters-in-law, Gertrudis and Juana, and Juana's baby. Almeron Dickinson, the hatmaker from Gonzales, brought his wife and little baby girl. About a dozen other Tejano women and children came, too. At this point there were only about 150 rebel soldiers at the Alamo. This was not nearly enough.

Right away Travis sent out two riders, one to Gonzales and the other to the fort in Goliad where

four hundred men were under the leadership of
James Fannin. Travis was asking for more troops.

At the same time Jim Bowie and a group of his
men searched the deserted shacks for food and
horses. By now it was becoming clear to Bowie's
men that their leader was not well—and that it
wasn't from drinking too much at the fandango.

By early evening on February 23, everyone inside the Alamo saw something terrifying. Gazing over its walls across the river, they watched Santa Anna raise a banner atop the church bell tower in Béxar. The banner was bloodred. It meant: no mercy.

Santa Anna couldn't wait to kill every Texian rebel who had defied his rule. Especially those at the Alamo, where Cós's men had been defeated and driven out.

This fury had driven Santa Anna north with six

thousand men in the winter. They had started out in late December 1835 on a march of more than 350 miles. There were not nearly enough supplies.

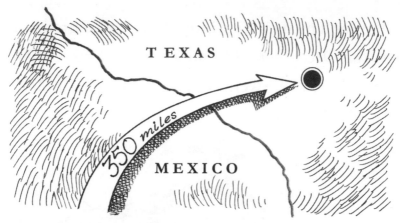

TEXAS

350 miles

MEXICO

Many of the men had been forced into the army. They did not want to be soldiers. On the long, tough march, many deserted. Some collapsed from lack of water or food, as did the horses, mules, and oxen. Some soldiers froze to death in the snow. Some were killed off by Comanche or

Apache raiders, who also stole their food.

By the time he reached Béxar, Santa Anna had lost between four hundred and five hundred men. He came into town ahead of most of his army. Still, at least fifteen hundred men were with him. Santa Anna was not worried. He also knew that the rest of the troops would catch up in the following days.

With Santa Anna was General Cós. He was eager for revenge after his earlier surrender to the rebels. General Sesma was in command of 160 deadly lancers on horseback. Everyone in Texas feared them. They could chase a man down and run him through with their sharp spears.

Many wives, girlfriends, and children of the soldiers had come on the long march, too. They slowed down the pace. Many of them died. But they were helpful as cooks and nurses. If Santa Anna had ordered them home, probably many of his troops would have followed after them.

By the time the enemy arrived, Jim Bowie was so weak that he handed over his command to William Travis. Travis ordered a shot blasted from the eighteen-pound cannon to show all the Mexican soldiers surrounding the fort that they were ready to fight.

The battle at the Alamo had begun.

CHAPTER 6
Help!

At this time, there were only about 150 rebels in the fort. From outside, the Mexicans kept firing their cannons at the weak adobe walls. In time the walls would fall. Then Santa Anna's troops could storm into the Alamo.

Help *had* to be on the way. They just needed to hold out until reinforcements came. This is what the rebels at the Alamo told themselves. Travis's letter to James Fannin at the fort in Goliad had stated the situation very clearly: "We have but little provisions, but enough to serve us till you and your men arrive."

Unfortunately, James Fannin was not a soldier with a love of battle. At Goliad, he'd been writing his own letters to the head of the temporary Texas government. "I am a better judge of my military abilities than others," he wrote, "and if I am qualified to command an Army, I have not found it out."

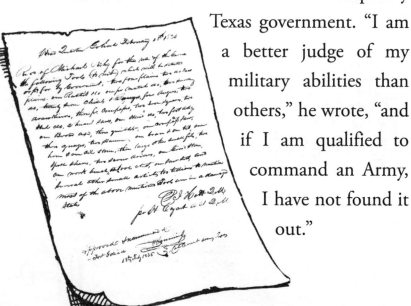

James Fannin

If William Travis had too much confidence in himself, James W. Fannin had too little. At Goliad, he was put in charge of four hundred men, the largest group of rebel soldiers in all Texas. Fannin didn't want the job. Over and over he wrote to the governor of Texas begging to be relieved of his position. "I *feel*, I *know* . . . that I am incompetent," he wrote. Fannin always regretted his failure to help when the men at the Alamo were in trouble. Fannin didn't have to live with the guilt for long. He was executed at Goliad by the Mexicans just a couple of weeks after the battle at the Alamo.

However, Fannin began to think that he'd better set out with some men to the Alamo. He left Goliad with cannons, ammunition, and oxen pulling supply wagons. However, within two hundred yards from town, some of the wagons broke down. Other wagons had a hard time crossing the San Antonio River. By nightfall, the men started to think about how little food they had, how cold it was, and how many Mexican soldiers there would be waiting at the Alamo.

What would happen to them if they fell into the
hands of Santa Anna's army? What would happen
to the undefended Goliad? Fannin and his men
turned around and headed back to Goliad. There
would be no help from Fannin.

Sam Houston didn't respond to Travis's request for help, either. He had heard that the rebels at the Alamo were outnumbered. But he didn't believe that the situation was nearly as bad as it actually was. There would be no help coming from Sam Houston.

Travis also wrote a letter to the people of Gonzales to come join the fight, and yet another letter that he wanted printed in newspapers. "Fellow citizens and compatriots," he wrote, "I am besieged by a thousand or more of the Mexicans under Santa Anna. . . . I shall never surrender or retreat. Then, I call on you in the name of Liberty, of patriotism & everything dear to the American character, to come to our aid." He signed the letter "Victory or death." Travis handed the letter to a rebel Texian who burst out of the main gate on his horse and slipped through the Mexican lines.

The letter got to San Felipe, where it was

printed on a handbill. Copies appeared all over
Texas. The letter eventually ran in newspapers

across the border in New Orleans, Louisiana, and as far away as New York City.

Finally, help came. Late one night, a group of

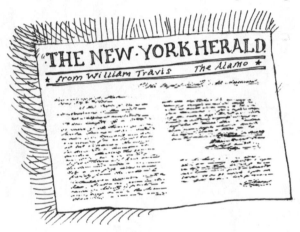

thirty-two men entered the fort. They had come from Gonzales. They were welcomed with wild cheering. These were the first reinforcements to arrive.

Unfortunately, they were also the last.

Although the rebels were small in number, General Santa Anna soon saw that they were not so easy to defeat.

On February 25, when Santa Anna led his first

attack on the fort's south wall, his men were driven back by Texas rifle fire and grapeshot. The rebels were becoming a personal embarrassment to His Excellency, as Santa Anna liked to be called.

As the siege continued day after day, everyone inside the walls tried to keep up their spirits. But it was hard. No one slept much, because Santa Anna's forces fired at them throughout the night. Mexican soldiers played bugle calls at all hours to make it

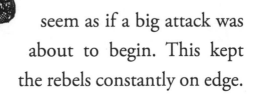

seem as if a big attack was about to begin. This kept the rebels constantly on edge.

And Jim Bowie was growing sicker and weaker. Sometimes, when he was strong enough, the men carried him to the long barracks, where he would encourage his boys to fight their hardest.

Travis understood that a big attack had to come soon. According to one story, he stopped in to see Almeron Dickinson's wife and little daughter.

While playing with the baby, he took off a ring
he wore. It was gold with a black cat's-eye stone.
He put the ring on a piece of string and placed it
around the baby's neck. He wanted her to have it
in case something happened to him.

The Ring

Although Angelina Dickinson was too young to remember the Alamo, she had William Travis's ring as a souvenir. As an adult she gave the ring to a friend who later fought in the Civil War. The ring was passed down in his family through the years until a Houston attorney donated it to the Alamo museum. Today the ring sits on display in the Alamo, where its original owner was killed.

During lulls in the cannon fire, David Crockett tried to cheer everyone up. He had a fiddle and liked to play country tunes on it. Another man who was originally from Scotland had brought along his set of bagpipes. The two sometimes had contests to see who could make the best music—or the most noise. The bagpipes always won the noise contests.

On March 5, the siege had been going on for twelve days. The Mexicans stopped their cannon fire in the afternoon, so it was finally quiet. Travis called all the men together. He told them he preferred to die for his country rather than surrender. Legend has it he drew a line in the dirt with his sword. Every man who wanted to stay and die with him should step across the line.

One by one the rebels crossed over to Travis's side of the line. Jim Bowie was carried on his cot. In the end, only one man—someone said to be named Louis Rose—remained on the far side of the line; he escaped over the north wall and reached the river—and safety.

Travis knew the situation was hopeless. So  he gave Robert Evans a secret order. When the fort was overrun by the Mexicans, Evans was to blow up the gunpowder stored in the front room of the church. At least the rebels would have the satisfaction of taking down as many enemy soldiers as possible.

It remained quiet all night. For the first time in weeks, everyone in the Alamo could sleep. Even the lookouts right outside the fort dozed off at their posts.

That was a terrible mistake.

The lookouts didn't hear the Mexican soldiers creeping up on them to slit their throats.

This was the beginning of the end.

A nineteenth-century engraving of Stephen F. Austin

An early twentieth-century photo of the Alamo

A mural inside the Gonzales Memorial Museum
depicting details of the Alamo

An engraving depicting Spanish missionaries at the Alamo

A photo of the Rio Grande

A nineteenth-century illustration
depicting the plan of the Alamo

The Travis "victory or death" letter

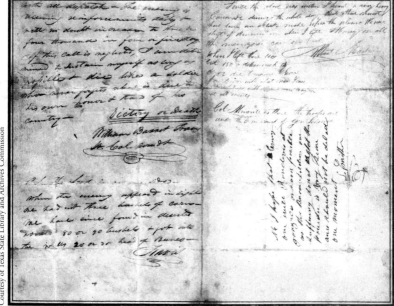

TEXAS
EXPECTS EVERY MAN TO DO HIS DUTY.

SAN FELIPE FEB. 28th 1836.

TO THE CITIZENS OF BRAZORIA

I send you by Express, the latest information from San Antonio, the Governor's call, and the proceedings of the meeting at San Felipe; from these you will learn, the necessity for your services, the call that is made upon you, and upon what your fellow citizens in this place are doing. I know that you will not be backward in affording your country the assistance that she demands. I advise all that live in the upper part of the Jurisdiction who can procure horses, to leave immediately for Gonzales, the remainder rendezvous at Velasco, on the 9th proximo; at which place and time, I have engaged Capt. Grayson to be ready with the steam boat Laura, to transport all who are disposed to assist their country to the westward. I consider it unnecessary to make an appeal to your patriotism, as the information from Bexar, speaks louder than words.

JOHN A. WHARTON,
Adjutant General.

Executive Department of Texas.

Fellow-Citizens of Texas:—
The enemy is upon us, a strong force warred on the Walls of San Antonio, and threatens that garrison with the sword. Our country imperiously demands the service of every patriotic arm, and longer to continue in a state of apathy will be criminal.

Citizens of Texas, descendants of Washington awake, arouse yourselves—The question is now to be decided. Are we to continue as freemen, or bow beneath the rod of military despotism, shall we without a struggle, sacrifice our fortune, our lives and our liberties, or shall we imitate the example of our forefathers and hurl destruction upon the heads of our oppressors; the eyes of the word are upon us, all friends of liberty and of the rights of men are anxious spectators of our conflict and deeply enlisted in our cause; shall we disappoint their hopes and expectations? No, let us at once fly to our arms, march to the battle field, meet the foe and give renewed evidence to the world that the sons of freemen, unlisted in defence of their rights and liberties are irresistible. "Now is the day and now is the hour," that Texas expects every man to do his duty. Let us show ourselves worthy to be free, and we will be free. Our brethren of the United States have, with a generosity and devotion to liberty, unparalleled in the annals of men, offered us every assistance. We have arms, ammunition, clothing and provisions; all we have to do, is to sustain ourselves for the present. Rest assured that succors will not permit the chains of slavery to be riveted on us.

Fellow-Citizens, your garrison at San Antonio is surrounded by more than twenty times their numbers. Will you see them perish by the hands of a mercenary soldiery, without an effort for their relief? They cannot sustain the seige more than thirty days; for the sake of humanity, before that time give them succor. Citizens of the east, your brethren of the Brazos and Colorado, expect your assistance, afford it, and check the march of the enemy and suffer not your own land to become the seat of war, without your immediate aid we cannot sustain the war. Fellow-Citizens, I call upon you as your executive officer to "turn out;" it is your country that demands your help. He who longer slumbers on the volcano must be a madman.

He who refuses to aid his country in this, her hour of peril and danger is a traitor. All persons able to bear arms in Texas are called on to rendezvous at the town of Gonzales, with the least possible delay armed and equipped for battle. *Our rights and liberties must be protected;* to the battle field march and save the country. An approving word smiles upon us, the God of battles is on our side, and victory awaits us.

Confidently believing that your energies will be sufficient for the occasion, and that your efforts will be ultimately successfully.

I subscribe myself your fellow-citizen,
HENRY SMITH, Gov'r.

TO THE CITIZENS OF TEXAS.
COMMANDANCY OF THE ALAMO, BEJAR Feb. 24th 1836.

Fellow-Citizens,

I am beseiged by a 1000 or more of the Mexicans under Santa Anna. I have sustained a continual bombardment and cannonade for 24 hours and have not lost a man. The enemy have demanded a surrender at discretion otherwise the garrison is to be put to the sword, if the fort is taken. I have answered the demand with the cannon shot. And our flag still waves proudly from the walls. I shall never surrender nor retreat; then I call on you in the name of *liberty*, of patriotism, & of every thing dear to the American character to come to our aid with all possible despatch; the enemy are receiving reinforcements daily, and will no doubt increase to 3 or 4000 in 4 or 5 days. Though this call may be neglected I am determined to sustain myself as long as possible and die like a soldier who never forgets what is due to his own honor and that of his country,
VICTORY OR DEATH.
W. B. TRAVIS,
Lieut. Col. Com'dt,

BRAZORIA, TEXAS

WEDNESDAY, MARCH 2, 1836

Want of room compels us to decline making any comments on the alarming situation which we occupy, we give the news received, and every man will be able to judge for himself.

Handbills will be published whenever occasion requires it; which will be a sure and expeditious mode of conveying information of our short. A handbill will be published tomorrow containing the news brought by today's mail.

MEETING
OF THE CITIZENS OF SAN FELIPE.

At a meeting of the citizens held in the town of San Felipe, on 28th February. Joseph Baker was unanimously called to the chair, and R. P. Cage appointed secretary. A communication from Wm. B. Travis, Lt. Col. Commandant of the post of Bejar, having been read, on the object of the meeting explained, on motion of Mosely B. dear Esq.

Resolved, That the Chairman appoint a committee of twelve to prepare an address and draft resolutions for the adoption of this meeting.

Whereupon The chairman appointed Mosely Baker, J. A. Wharton, F. J. Starr, J. R. Jones, W. R. Hensley, A. Ewing, P. B. Dexter, J. Fletcher, J. W. Crane and Thos. Gay. The meeting adjourned to 8 o'clock.

The meeting again assembled at 11 o'clock, when the address and resolutions were reported and unanimously adopted.

To our fellow citizens.

The undersigned having been appointed by a meeting of citizens of San Felipe, on this day, with the accompanying commandment of Bejar and to this as may issued. You must arm yourselves, and march with all delay to the field to the western breeze the flag haloo and you will shield and will children of Gonzales and the last agonizing will follow. Citizens and Brazos, your wives and your homes are also your families destroyed be enslaved; and you resort to the field of abandon your information shall be ted, the blood of have crimsoned the of many a devoted you.

Inhabitants of the citizens of the west

Newspaper coverage of Travis's "victory or death" letter

TO THE CITIZENS OF TEXAS.
COMMANDANCY OF THE ALAMO, BEJAR Feb. 24th 1836.

Fellow-Citizens.

I am beseiged by a 1000 or more of the Mexicans under Santa Anna. I have sustained a continual bombardment and cannonade for 24 hours and have not lost a man. The enemy have demanded a surrender at discretion otherwise the garrison is to be put to the sword, if the fort is taken. I have answered the demand with the cannon shot. And our flag still waves proudly from the walls. I shall never surrender nor retreat; then I call on you in the name of *liberty*, of patriotism, & of every thing dear to the American character to come to our aid with all possible despatch; the enemy are receiving reinforcements daily, and will no doubt increase to 3 or 4000 in 4 or 5 days. Though this call may be neglected I am determined to sustain myself as long as possible and die like a soldier who never forgets what is due to his own honor and that of his country,
VICTORY OR DEATH.
W. B. TRAVIS,
Lieut. Col. Com'dt,

A print of the Alamo from a sketch by a
government draftsman, dated March 23, 1861

An engraving of the fall of the Alamo, from about 1895

A map of Texas created by Stephen F. Austin in 1835

The only known painting of
Jim Bowie done from life

A portrait of
William B. Travis

A photo from inside the Alamo chapel

A nineteenth-century
photo of Sam Houston

A portrait of
Davy Crockett

A painting depicting the surrender of Santa Anna

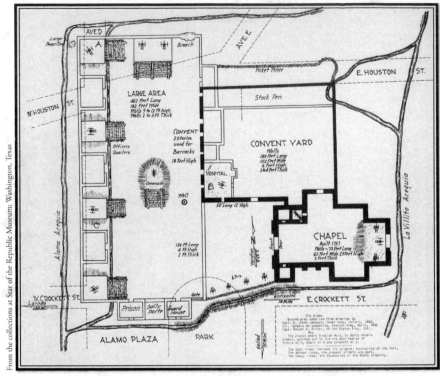

Map of the Alamo showing the "ground plan"
compiled from drawings in 1826

A postcard of the "ruins of the historical Alamo"

A photo of Alamo Plaza, taken in the late 1870s

A photo of the Alamo Cenotaph, a monument erected in Alamo Plaza in 1939

A postcard of Alamo Plaza, Texas, from 1917

A recent photo of Alamo Plaza at night

CHAPTER 7
Attack

No one knows for sure exactly what happened in the Alamo the early morning of March 6 before dawn. But the rough story has been pieced together from the few eyewitness accounts and from evidence. At around 3:00 a.m. the Mexican soldiers began sneaking up to the old mission.

Although the night was cold, Santa Anna had ordered them to leave their coats and blankets behind. This way they could move quickly and quietly. By 5:30 a.m. the sleeping Texian lookouts lay dead at their feet.

The Mexican bugler sounded the charge to attack. So many times before, the bugle call was a false alarm to frighten the rebels. This time it was for real!

All at once Mexican soldiers rushed at the Alamo. Inside the fort, a Texian threw open the door to Travis's room and shouted, "The Mexicans are coming!"

Travis jumped out of bed and grabbed his double-barreled shotgun and sword. He ran into the courtyard with his slave, Joe, behind him. It was still dark. Rebels came pouring out of the barracks and granary buildings. Gunners ran to the cannons. From the other side of the wall came a horrible rumble—it was the sound of thousands of enemy feet running toward the fort walls. The north wall was easy to climb up. Logs that reinforced it provided toeholds for the enemy. The Alamo was no longer under siege—it was under direct attack.

"Come on, boys, the Mexicans are upon us!" shouted Travis, eager to fight at last.

The Texians aimed their cannons at the oncoming troops. Many soldiers were killed. But others had already reached the wall and were out of range of the cannons. So rebel riflemen shot down at them. Travis leaned over the parapet and aimed his shotgun. He fired only one round before a bullet hit him in the forehead. Instantly he fell down dead. His shotgun toppled below. Joe managed to find safety in one of the rooms along the west wall.

Still more Mexican soldiers came climbing over the north wall. On the west side of the fort, General Cós's men bashed in the walls with picks and axes, then stormed inside.

On the east side, another column of soldiers, row after row, were advancing on the compound.

Rifle fire from Texians on the roof of the chapel managed to push them back. Mexican soldiers farther back kept firing, but with all the smoke and confusion, they often hit their own comrades.

Still another Mexican force had managed to storm the Alamo's main gate to the south, but there, too, Texian cannon fire held them back.

Close by the church, a cannon sat on a platform with few men to defend it. The Texians rushed to spike the cannon. That meant blocking the hole so it couldn't fire anymore. But they were overpowered by enemy troops already inside the fort, and the cannon was taken by the Mexicans.

As for David Crockett, no one knows for sure how he met his death.

One story has it that he and his Tennessee boys were stationed by the palisade (the fence made of wooden stakes with sharpened points).

From there they kept firing their rifles, taking down as many of the enemy as they could. No one was a better shot than David Crockett!

Almeron Dickinson blasted the cannon from the top of the church. Inside, his wife and the other women and children stayed huddled, fearful for their lives.

Over the noise of battle and the shouts of dying men came the sound of another bugle call. Santa Anna was sending in his best and fiercest troops. They, too, were greeted by cannon fire from the rebels. It didn't stop them. They pushed ahead to the wall, climbed over, and joined the other Mexican troops inside the Alamo.

The Mexicans were now coming at the Texians from every side.

CHAPTER 8
Overrun

Nearly all the Texians still alive were now inside the church and barracks. One small group of men managed to wheel a cannon around and fire on enemy troops inside the fort. Then a moment later these rebels were cut down by Mexican gunfire.

Near the main gate, Jim Bowie lay on his cot. For probably the only time in his life, he hadn't been able to join the fight.

The fort was overrun. The Texians didn't even have time to reload their rifles. So they beat at soldiers with rifle butts, bayonets, axes, even the ramrods used to load the cannons. When all else failed, they used their bare fists to fight off the enemy. But there were too many.

Almeron Dickinson was still firing from the roof of the church. Now he jumped down and ran inside to the women and children. "Great God, Sue, the Mexicans are inside our walls," he said to his wife, Susannah. "All is lost. If they spare you, save my child." He kissed Susannah and the baby and ran out. Susannah never saw her husband again.

Did any of the men inside the Alamo escape from the fort?

Yes.

Were they fleeing to safety or hoping to fight the Mexicans another day?

That is not entirely clear.

About sixty-two men managed to slip out through the small wooden gate at the east end of the palisade. They ran toward the hills in the direction of the town of Gonzales. But Santa Anna had expected some rebels would try to get away. General Sesma had 375 soldiers on horseback waiting for them in a long curved line.

They attacked the Texians with their lances and sabers. Within moments the escaping rebels were dead.

Back inside the fort, Mexican soldiers searched every room in the Alamo, shooting, stabbing, or clubbing the Texians to death. In the frenzy, Mexican soldiers killed each other by accident. Even the barracks cat was cornered and killed. "It's not a cat!" the soldiers shouted. "It's an American!"

At the church, Robert Evans raced toward the powder magazine. He meant to follow Travis's orders to blow up the Alamo. But he was cut down before reaching the gunpowder. He died on the floor of the church, which was already slippery with blood.

The battle was over in about an hour and a half. The number of Mexican soldiers who died is uncertain. Accounts say between 400 and 600 men. All the Alamo defenders—about 183

men—were dead. Among the few survivors were
Susannah Dickinson and her baby, an eleven-
year-old boy named Enrique Esparza, and Travis's
slave, Joe.

As the sun rose, Santa Anna came through the
main gate to view the battle scene—piles of twisted
bodies and blood. Joe was ordered to point out
William Travis, David Crockett, and Jim Bowie.

Legend has it that Santa Anna found Jim with a Bowie knife in one hand, a pistol in the other. All around him were the bodies of Mexican soldiers. Had Bowie killed them before being killed himself? It's unlikely. However, this is certainly the way Jim Bowie would want to be remembered.

Santa Anna had achieved his victory. But one of his officers remarked about the bloody day, "With another victory like this one we may all end up in hell."

Jim Bowie's mother received the news of her son's death bravely. She said that she was sure that "no wounds were found in his back." (By that she meant that he had never tried to run away from the enemy.) Then she returned to her housework.

Sad News

The news of David Crockett's death was brought to his family in Tennessee. His wife, Elizabeth, had stood on the porch every night after David had left for the Alamo. With her hand shading her eyes, she'd look west, hoping for his return. Now she knew that was not going to happen. In 1838, David's son Robert set off for Texas for the Crockett land claim. Years later Elizabeth made the trip as well. When she died, a monument was erected at her grave.

CHAPTER 9
Remember the Alamo

With the battle over, Santa Anna's orders were that the bodies of his dead soldiers be taken to the cemetery on the west side of town. There they were buried.

As for the rebels, did Santa Anna treat them with the same respect?

No.

The bodies of the rebels were placed on wooden pyres outside the fort. In the late afternoon a torch set the pyres on fire. They burned for two days. Thousands of vultures circled the smoky sky above, waiting to feast on the burned remains. Almost a year later, on February 25, 1837, ashes were still found on the site and given an official funeral.

Soon after the Alamo's fall, there was another blow to the Texian cause for independence. It happened at Goliad, the fort near the Alamo. James Fannin had not gone to help the men at the Alamo. Now he was given orders to blow up

Goliad. Better to destroy Goliad than to let Santa Anna take control of it.

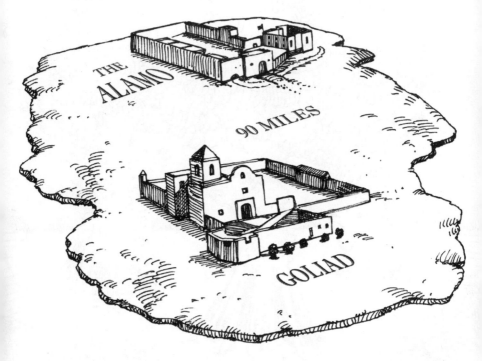

Fannin was not a man who acted quickly. But finally, he had the cannons spiked and the wagons loaded full of ammo. Then everything was set ablaze.

Fannin and his men headed east, where unfortunately they were stopped by Mexican troops and forced to surrender. The Mexican general promised that, as prisoners of war, Fannin and his men would be treated with honor. They were marched back to what was left of Goliad.

Perhaps the Mexican general meant to keep his word. But Santa Anna was not about to show mercy. The next morning Fannin's men were divided into four groups. Each was given a different false story of where they were being led. A half mile from the fort, they were either shot or else stabbed to death with a bayonet or lance.

Somehow twenty-eight men escaped to tell the tale.

Fannin was the last to die. And he died bravely. He had three requests: He wanted to be shot in the heart, he wanted his pocket watch returned to his widow, and he wanted a decent burial. Instead, he was shot in the face. A Mexican officer kept his pocket watch. His body was thrown on a pyre and burned.

The massacre of over four hundred men at Goliad, coming so soon after the Alamo, lit a fire in the hearts of Texians—and Americans. The terrible events brought Texians together in a way that nothing had before. The rebels at the Alamo were seen as brave heroes who had died for freedom.

On April 21, less than two months after the fall of the Alamo, Santa Anna's fifteen-hundred-man army was surprised by a force of nine hundred Texians led by Sam Houston. The fighting took place near the San Jacinto River. The Mexicans had not expected a Texian attack during the day in open territory. Then suddenly a fife and drum struck up a tune, and the rebels rushed forward with cries of "Remember the Alamo!"

The Mexicans were caught unprepared. Some desperately cried, "Me no Alamo!" ("I wasn't at the Alamo!") But the Texians would not be stopped. They were bent on avenging the Alamo. Goliad, too. According to Sam Houston, the battle lasted all of eighteen minutes. The Mexicans lost 630, with 200 wounded. Only nine Texians were killed that day, and only thirty wounded.

The afternoon of the following day, the Texians captured a man in shabby clothes hiding in the tall grass. When he was brought back to camp, the Mexican prisoners shouted, "El Presidente!" The Texians were amazed: Here was Santa Anna himself!

Santa Anna

It's not surprising that Antonio López de Santa Anna was hated by Texian rebels. But he also was hated by many of his own people in Mexico. And yet, although he was sent into exile several times, somehow he'd manage to return to Mexico and seize control of the government again.

After the defeat at San Jacinto, he lived in exile in the United States until 1837. In 1838, he led the army against invading French forces. He lost his leg in the fighting—and had it buried with full military honors! Santa Anna died penniless and alone in 1876.

Many Texians wanted to kill Santa Anna right away. But Houston, who had been wounded in the fighting, wasn't about to get rid of someone as valuable as Santa Anna. He proposed to let the general go on the promise that all Mexican troops leave Texas at once and for good. Santa Anna agreed. His army retreated across the Rio Grande. Many of the soldiers were all too glad to go home. It was fine with them if they never returned to what was now the free Republic of Texas.

Despite the terrible defeat at the Alamo, the courage of that band of men inspired others to fight on and win freedom from Mexico. Their bravery is why the Alamo will always be known as "the cradle of Texas liberty."

Republic Of Texas

The Republic of Texas existed from March 2, 1836, to February 19, 1846. It included all of present-day Texas and parts of what today are Oklahoma, Kansas, Wyoming, Colorado, and New Mexico.

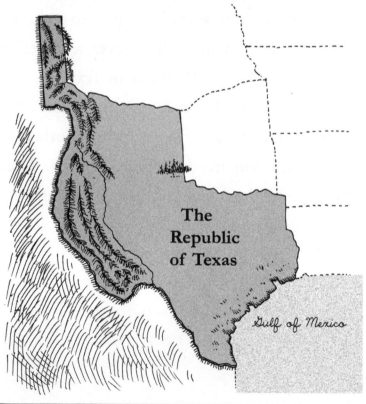

The
Republic
of Texas

Gulf of Mexico

The republic never had enough money to govern itself properly. People began to talk about the republic being annexed by—or becoming part of—the United States. The United States would pay all of Texas's debts in return. On October 13, 1845, a large majority in Texas voted to accept the offer. Texas became the twenty-eighth state on December 29, 1845. Its state flag is the flag of the Republic of Texas and gives Texas its nickname, the Lone Star State.

Timeline of the Alamo

1821	Stephen F. Austin arrives in San Antonio on August 3
1830	April 6, Mexican Congress passes the Law of 1830, forbidding US immigrants from settling in Texas
1833	General Antonio López de Santa Anna becomes president of Mexico
1834	Stephen F. Austin is thrown in jail after asking the Mexican government to allow Texas to become an independent state under Mexican rule
1835	December 5, the battle in Béxar begins, and the Army of the People fights for the Alamo against the Mexican Army
1836	February 8, David Crockett arrives with volunteers to help defend the Alamo
Mar 2	Texas Declaration of Independence is approved; Republic of Texas is declared
Mar 6	The Alamo falls in a bloody attack before dawn; William B. Travis, David Crockett, and Jim Bowie are killed
1845	December 29, Texas becomes the twenty-eighth US state
1846	United States declares war on Mexico
1848	The Treaty of Guadalupe-Hidalgo ends the Mexican-American War

Timeline of the World

Mexico wins independence from Spain — 1821
California becomes Mexican territory
US president James Monroe — 1823
declares the Monroe Doctrine
The first US railway is constructed in Massachusetts — 1826
Joseph Smith publishes *The Book of Mormon* — 1830
Slavery is banned in the British Empire — 1833
Victoria becomes the queen of Great Britain — 1837
Charles Goodyear discovers vulcanization of rubber — 1839
Charles Dickens's book *A Christmas Carol* is published — 1843
First "official" telegraph sent from — 1844
Washington, DC, to Baltimore, Maryland
Potato famine begins in Ireland — 1845
The planet Neptune is discovered — 1846
The first women's rights conference — 1848
is held at Seneca Falls, New York
Uncle Tom's Cabin by Harriet — 1851
Beecher Stowe is published

Bibliography

*Books for young readers

Davis, William C. *Three Roads to the Alamo: The Lives and Fortunes of David Crockett, James Bowie, and William Barret Travis*. New York: HarperCollins Publishers, 1998.

Donovan, James. *The Blood of Heroes: The 13-Day Struggle for the Alamo—and the Sacrifice That Forged a Nation*. New York: Little, Brown and Company, 2012.

Harrigan, Stephen. **"Phil Collins Remembers the Alamo."** *American History*, April 2012.

*Murphy, Jim. *Inside the Alamo*. New York: Delacorte Press, 2003.

Tucker, Phillip Thomas. *Exodus From the Alamo: The Anatomy of the Last Stand Myth*. Havertown, PA: Casemate Publishers, 2010.

*Walker, Paul Robert. *Remember the Alamo: Texians, Tejanos, and Mexicans Tell Their Stories*. Washington, DC: National Geographic, 2007.

Websites

The Alamo. http://www.thealamo.org/.